Mark Zupo

100 Quotes I Live By

Words of Wisdom and Insight to Guide You through Life

By

Mark Zupo

Zupo, Mark

100 Quotes I Live By

Words of Wisdom and Insight to
Guide You through Life

 Printed in the United States of America.

ISBN-13: 978-0983994534 (Mark Zupo)

ISBN-10: 0983994536

Library of Congress catalog Card #

Also available in Audio CD format

To order, contact:

1-678-640-0585

www.MarkZupo.com

Slippery Rock Press Publishing™

DEDICATION

This book is dedicated to my brother Chris. The example of his success and determination shines the way for me to find my way.

"Own your dreams and plan your success."
Mark Zupo - 2010

ABOUT THE AUTHOR

Mark Zupo is an "Accomplished Entrepreneur" who has devoted his life to helping others succeed in their goals and dreams. His goal is to help you fulfill your career goals and achieve financial freedom and independence by building the successful..."Business of You!"

Mark Zupo is a dynamic and insightful speaker, recognized for his empowering and motivational focus to your success. As a driven leader with a commanding presence, he motivates, inspires, energizes and empowers his audience.

Mark has been the driving force in changing the lives of anyone within range of his voice. Mark's "3-Foot Rule" makes him one of the most sought-after speakers in his industry.

Mark's speaking career in industry spans 25 years and he has delivered more-than, 1,200 presentations. From his experiences he has authored and co-authored many books on self-development, business development techniques and marketing enterprises.

Commitment

"Commitment is what transforms a promise into reality. It is the words that speak boldly of your intentions. And the actions that speak louder than the words. It is making the time when there is none and coming through time after time after time, year after year after year. Commitment is the stuff character is made of; the power to change the face of things. It is the daily triumph of integrity over skepticism."

- Unknown

CONTENTS

PERSPECTIVE

...A way of regarding situations, facts, etc., and judging their relative importance.

We live in a world that is kind and cruel, happy and sad.

We are surrounded by optimism and pessimism.

Both are irrefutable and it would be unrealistic to suggest that by thinking only about warm things, cold ones will cease to exist.

Expanding your perspective isn't about denying reality or adopting a "Pollyanna" way of looking at life.

It's about choosing a viewpoint, attitude or mindset that is most likely to promote happiness and help you achieve the life you desire.

Each of our lives is filled with joy and sorrow and each of us chooses how we relate to that which causes either.

Altering one's perspective is not a requirement—

it's an option.

"There is no burnt rice to a hungry person."

-Philippine Proverb

"At high tide the fish eat ants; at low tide the ants eat fish."

-Thai Proverb

"I never ask God to give me anything;

I only ask him to put me
where things are.

-Mexican Proverb

"Won't you come into the garden? I would like my roses to see you."

-Richard Brinsley Sheridan

"A man should never be ashamed to own he has been in the wrong, which is but saying... that he is wiser today than he was yesterday."

-Alexander Pope

"You don't have to be nuts...
Just the right kind of nuts!"

- Uncle Ed

FORGIVENESS

Willingness to forgive —to cease to blame or hold resentment

The act of forgiveness is a purposeful undertaking that releases the giver and receiver from being prisoners of the past.

There is no future in the past.

Without forgiveness, both given and received, our souls cannot know peace or harmony —and the freedom they afford.

Forgiveness is not something we have to do but rather something we allow to flow through us.

It doesn't require strength—only courage.

We must follow nature's lead and shed that which no longer serves us.

We must prune back that which doesn't produce bounty—so that it may grow again.

We must include ourselves among those we give the gift of forgiveness.

"Forgiveness is the fragrance the violet sheds on the heel that has crushed it."

-Mark Twain

"He who cannot forgive breaks the bridge over which he himself must pass."

-George Herbert

"Forgiveness does not change the past,
But it does enlarge the future."

-Paul Boese

"I can forgive, but I cannot forget, is only another way of saying, I will not forgive."

-Henry Ward Beecher

"Forgiveness is me giving up my right to hurt you for hurting me."

-Anonymous

"You deserve to be rich"

- Uncle Ed

LEADERSHIP

An act or instance of leading; providing guidance or direction

Power, the authority to direct someone or the ability to provide someone a paycheck does not equal leadership.

True leadership inspires its followers to *want* to achieve big goals. It influences them to do great things.

Effective leaders must have their followers trust and confidence. They must always be aware that their actions tell those who follow who they really are.

Leadership clarifies purpose and assures people they are an asset and a valuable resource.

It fosters creativity and makes it possible for those they lead to see their own potential and flourish under the vision and implementation of a common goal.

One does not have to own a business or be wealthy to practice the art of leadership.

Our lives are full of opportunities to demonstrate good leadership skills among our friends, family and peers each and every day.

"The best executive is the one who has sense enough to pick good men to do what he wants done, and self-restraint enough to keep from meddling with them while they do it."

-Theodore Roosevelt

"You do not lead by hitting people over the head.

That's assault, not leadership."

-Dwight D. Eisenhower

"What chance gathers she easily scatters. A great person attracts great people and knows how to hold them together."

-Johann Wolfgang Von Goethe

"It is absurd that a man should rule others, who cannot rule himself."

-Latin Proverb

"If your actions inspire others to dream more, learn more, do more and become more, you are a leader."

-John Quincy Adams

"Leaders must be close enough to relate to others, but far enough ahead to motivate them."

- John C. Maxwell

"A leader is best when people barely know he exists, when his work is done, his aim fulfilled, they will say: we did it ourselves."

—Lao Tzu

"Before you are a leader, success is all about growing yourself. When you become a leader, success is all about growing others."

—Jack Welch

"A great person attracts great people and knows how to hold them together."

—Johann Wolfgang Von Goethe

"A leader takes people where they want to go. A great leader takes people where they don't necessarily want to go, but ought to be. "

—Rosalynn Carter

"A true leader has the confidence to stand alone, the courage to make tough decisions, and the compassion to listen to the needs of others. He does not set out to be a leader, but becomes one by the equality of his actions and the integrity of his intent."

—Douglas MacArthur

"If your actions inspire others to dream more, learn more, do more and become more, you are a leader."

—John Quincy Adams

"Management is efficiency in climbing the ladder of success; leadership determines whether the ladder is leaning against the right wall."

—Stephen Covey

"Chin up, Chest out, Shoulders back and Eyes forward. Now you may take the first step."

Mark Zupo

HAPPINESS

A state of delight, pleasure or contentedness

Happiness is more than a pleasant moment or an agreeable sensation.

It is a way of being and of relating to the circumstances and events of your life. It transcends your momentary and your life-long conditions.

Happiness is a choice and a discipline—that defines the manner in which you experience your world.

Authentic and enduring happiness is contingent on internal matters rather than external situations. It is derived from cultivating inner peace and strength.

Practicing the art of happiness sets you free—not from experiencing negative emotions—but from being enslaved by them.

"The foolish man seeks happiness in the distance; the wise grows it under his feet."

-James Openheim

"Most folks are about as happy as they make up their minds to be."

-Abraham Lincoln

"We tend to forget that happiness doesn't come as a result of getting something we don't have, but rather of recognizing and appreciating what we do have."

-Frederick Keonig

"The best vitamin to be a happy person is B1."

-Author Unknown

“He is rich or poor according to what he is, not according to what he has.”

-Henry Ward Beecher

"Some cause happiness wherever they go...others cause happiness whenever they go"

Oscar Wilde

"It is not how much we choose to have that will make us happy, it is what we do with what we already have that will keep us happy."

Mark Zupo

"Money can't buy happiness but it can make you awful comfortable while you suffer being miserable."

Claire Boothe Luce

" With pain, hardship, discomfort and angst comes the definition of happiness as the measure against them."

Mark Zupo

SUCCESS

The favorable outcome of something attempted

Society's idea of success often begins and ends in the amount of money and power one acquires.

But in reality, success is a multifaceted concept defined by each of us based on personal goals and desires. And that doesn't always begin and end in finances.

It is true money is beneficial and affords one the luxury of making choices and most importantly the ability to say, no.

But financial successful alone can't buy love, happiness, friendship, peace or health.

To achieve a meaningful sense of personal pride and accomplishment, success must be measured by our own standards and encompass something other than the superficial admiration of others.

When we create a clear understanding of what success means to each of us in terms of personal relationships, business and moral matters we are capable of extracting a deep and satisfying meaning from life.

"One secret of success in life is for a man to be ready for his opportunity when it comes."

-Benjamin Disraeli

"Success is dependent on effort."

-Sophocles

"There is only one success-

To be able to spend your life in your own way."

-Christopher Morley

"Men are born to succeed, not fail."

-Henry David Thoreau

"Many of life's failures are people who did not realize how close they were to success when they gave up."

-Thomas Edison

"A goal without a plan is just a wish."

Antoine de Saint-Exupery

French writer (1900 - 1944)

"Develop products that fill your wallet not your garage."

Mark Zupo

"The difference between failure and success is a combination of effort, support and accountability."

Mark Zupo

"Your story is your success."

Mark Zupo

"No-one can tell the story of you better than you!"

Mark Zupo

"From anonymity to celebrity!"
"From obstacles to opportunity."

Mark Zupo

"People have to train their entire life just for an opportunity to compete in the Olympics! Just to compete one time!"

Mark Zupo

"The sky is always blue."

Mark Zupo

"Run fast before they move the finish line!"

Mark Zupo

"Don't be a Winner...
Be THE Winner!"

Mark Zupo

"You can't sell what people don't want...
People must want what you have to sell!"

Mark Zupo

"A whisper is heard louder than
screaming!"

Mark Zupo

Life

To give life is to live life.

What determines the root of life is the meaning we attach to it. Its value is represented in the legacy left behind and in the memories of those who we touched along the way. To be alive is to live. To support life we must help other live. It is to pursue a positive and satisfying experience of existence that is shared with others.

The remnants of human memory are the seeds of life that continue to grow and shed he future opportunities for relevance and significance. If we are to live we are to be significant to one's self and to those around us. Otherwise, we fail to be alive let alone to live.

"You can have anything you see with a
plan and action
providing you put your plan into action!"

Mark Zupo

"In order for your book to be successful,
you have to remember three things...
Marketing!, Marketing!, Marketing!"

Mark Zupo

"A book isn't just writing and reading, its 10% book and 90% marketing!"

Mark Zupo

"If it doesn't make money... it doesn't make sense!"

Mark Zupo

"Knowledge combined with action...
has produced more millionaires...
than all the tea in China!"

Unknown

"The best way to fail...
is never to try!"

Unknown

"100% of the products you don't have for sale...
will assuredly never make you any money!"

Mark Zupo

"If you believe in your heart all that your mind can conceive,
it will dictate your ability to achieve every success."

Mark Zupo

"Write a Book:

: Establishes Your Credibility

: Projects Your Authority

: Promotes Your Visibility"

Mark Zupo

"It's like trying to stuff two gallons of milk into a one gallon jug."

Mark Zupo

"Things will work out in the end; and if they haven't,
you're not to the end yet."

(Unknown)

"The bad thing about being in business for your-self is...

You're in business for yourself!

The good thing about being in business for yourself is...

You're in business for yourself!"

Mark Zupo

"Entrepreneurs do more with less.
They do everything with nothing.
They expect little from anyone and
demands everything from themselves."

Mark Zupo

"When I was given work to do they asked me to do more,

When I did more they gave me more.

When I asked for help because I had too much to do, they told me to do more with less.

When I did more with less,

They expected me to do more with less than I had to do before I was given more to do to begin with!

Then...when I couldn't do any more, they fired me because I couldn't do my job!"

Mark Zupo

‘Need not greed.”

Mark Zupo

“Entrepreneurs are the highest order of life: Success-Driven, Goal-Focused, Achievement-Determined, Purpose-Intent animal on the planet."

Mark Zupo

"My Master Plan"

Vision = Direction

Direction = Action

Action = Results

Results= Focus

Focus = Success!"

Mark Zupo

"System-ate

Automate

Delegate

Replicate"

Mark Zupo

‘Part-time work for

Full-time income.”

Tom Antion

"My Goal.........

My Purpose........

My Dream...............

My Focus......................."

Mark Zupo

"Most people work harder to make a living, than they ever will to make money!"

Mark Zupo

"If It's to be,

It's up to Me!"

Joe Sabah

"3-Keys to Success:

Do Something - Write About it

And Sell it!"

Mark Zupo

"Anytime two or more people gather together,
One should be a teacher and the others...a student."

Joe Sabah

"People don't buy Features,

They Buy Benefits."

Mark Zupo

My success lies in the rule of 3...M.S.I.

"Multiple Streams of Income."

Mark Zupo

"Ideas are a Dime-a-Dozen,

Actions are More Rare than Diamonds."

Mark Zupo

"Every challenge is an opportunity,

Every opportunity is a gift,

The greater the challenge, the greater the opportunity."

Mark Zupo

"The power in character isn't built from adversity or difficult experiences,

It lays a hidden strength concealed like the energy stored I gunpowder... revealing itself when ignited."

Mark Zupo

"Nobody can sell you...like you."

Mark Zupo

"The solution – Riches start in the mind, not in the bank!"

Mark Zupo

"You start to grow when you are forced to stretch. If you're not growing you're dying."

Mark Zupo

"Start where you stand.'

Napoleon Hill

"Make your life your business and your business your life."

Mark Zupo

"Live an extraordinary life to achieve extraordinary results."

Mark Zupo

"Great leaders come from great students."

Mark Zupo

"Turbo-charge your life by creating your destiny on demand."

Mark Zupo

"The greater the challenge the greater the opportunity."

Mark Zupo

"Anytime two or more people get together, one should be a teacher and the other the student"

Mark Zupo

My Business Is My Life! My Life Is My Business!

Mark Zupo

"Make your mess your message!"

Mark Zupo

"Success is not a matter of ability

but rather

A product of willingness."

Mark Zupo

"A goal without a plan is a dream

That won't come through."

Mark Zupo

"If it is to be...

It is up to me."

William H. Johnsen

"Ordinary people do extraordinary things by taking

extraordinary steps to achieve extraordinary results."

Mark Zupo

"Only speak or write on a subject you have earned the right to speak or write on. Therefore I choose genius!"

Dale Carnegie / Mark Zupo

"Anytime two or more people gather together,
One should be a teacher and the other the student."

Joe Sabah

"Ideas are a dime a dozen,

The people who put them into action are priceless."

Joe Sabah

"Every challenge is an opportunity,

The bigger the challenge...the greater the opportunity."

Mark Zupo

"If you don't build your dream then someone else will hire you to help build theirs."

Dhirubhai Ambani

"Make Money, Save Money,

Save Time, Avoid Pain, Be Happy."

Mark Zupo

"I don't know what your destiny will be, but one thing I do know: the only ones among you who will be really happy are those

who have sought and found how to serve."

Albert Schweitzer

"The market doesn't determine your success...the market determines your strategy."

Mark Zupo

"Fear equals Opportunity."

Mark Zupo

"The best thing about entrepreneurship is that you are your own boss...The worst thing about entrepreneurship is that you are your own boss!"

Mark Zupo

"...The Bank of ME."

Mark Zupo

"Your lifestyle should govern your business not your business governing your lifestyle."

Mark Zupo

"It's not the aptitude it's the attitude,

It's not the IQ it's the I will,
It's not how much smarts you have,

it's how much heart you have."

Unknown

"Nay sayers say YOU never will...
the I Say-ers say I always will."

Mark Zupo

"Team work makes the dream work."

Unknown

"We get what we expect..."

Unknown

"Adversity is the best University...the best lessons learned are the hardest lessons earned!"

Mark Zupo

"People do not care about how much you know until they know how much you care!"

Mark Zupo

"The right attitude gets the right results."

Mark Zupo

"Rejection builds strength through experience."

Mark Zupo

"Purpose, Persistence, Passion, Priorities POWER!"

Mark Zupo

"If you can't listen then you can't glisten

If you don't know then you can't glow

If you believe you can achieve."

Mark Zupo

"We are people people...care more about those you meet than about yourself

Live closer to who you are than who you want to be."

Mark Zupo

"Genuineness, Honesty, Integrity

Generosity, Faith"

Mark Zupo

"You can't fail if you never try, you can't succeed if you never learn how not to fail."

Mark Zupo

"Sharing is the key...passion is the path."

Mark Zupo

"Edison tried 5,000 light bulbs...

Lincoln failed more than 35 times before becoming president. You will succeed because you want to!"

Mark Zupo

"...someone always wins!
IT MIGHT AS WELL BE YOU."

Mark Zupo

"You have to buy in to it...to own it."

Mark Zupo

"Own it...live it...believe it...teach it."

Mark Zupo

To achieve success,

"You must want it more than air..."

Mark Zupo

"The best achievers are the best students."

Mark Zupo

"Change is a door that can only be opened from the inside."

Chinese Proverb

"People behave towards you how they perceive you to be, not who you think you are."

Mark Zupo

"The bigger your mess...the bigger your message."

John F. Kennedy

"Life (and business) is like an EKG...there are ups and downs and that is a GOOD thing. Flat lines are dead. Life's challenges deliver ups and downs."

Mark Zupo

"You can't have a testimony until you've had a test."

Gary Eby

"We catch people's emotions like we catch their colds."

Mark Zupo

"We are most like the five people we are closest to."

Jim Rohn

"Intention

Attention

No Tension!"

Mark Zupo

The more I have the happier I'll be.

I'll be happy when.......I'll be happier.

Future fulfillment is a poor plan."

Mark Zupo

"Success doesn't bring happiness...

Happiness brings success."

Mark Zupo

"Passion delivers purpose.

Make your passion...your purpose!"

Mark Zupo

"The hole that you give through is the same hole that you receive through..."

Mark Zupo

Don't fill your ego...fill your bank account!

James Malinchak

If you are nearsighted...only see close in? you cannot see opportunity in vast universe. E.g.: put a penny close to your eye and a $100 dollar bill behind it. You cannot see the bigger amount for seeing only the penny.

Mark Zupo

"You Have To Teach People to Give You Money!"

Mark Zupo

"Your Life is Big Business!

And...No-one Ever Taught You How To Run It!"

Mark Zupo

"You have to sometimes set unrealistic goals to achieve realistic results."

Mark Zupo

"It's not your IQ

It's Your, "I will!"

Larry Price

"If You Have a speech...write it down...

you have a book.

If you have a book...market it...

you have credibility.

If you have credibility...protect it...

you have income for life."

Mark Zupo

"It's not How Much Smarts You Have

It's How Much Heart You Have."

James Malinchak

"Some Will,

Some Won't,

So What.........!"

Tony Cole

"Perfection is the Lowest Standard of Achievement...

DOING is the highest!"

Mark Zupo

"Celebrate Every Day:

You woke up

You can get up

You can earn a living

You can help someone else earn a living."

Mark Zupo

"The NET Value of money:

Money gets you what you want

Drives you to success

Forms desire to acquire it

Determines what you would do to get it."

Mark Zupo

"Measure everything you do.

Compare everything you measure to other's successes."

Mark Zupo

"What do I expect from today?
What did I make happened today?
What did I learn from today?
What will I do tomorrow?"
Mark Zupo

"Believe in your goals
Temper your mood
Develop your attitude
Dump your baggage."
Mark Zupo

"The greatest expression of

success is demonstrated at the Bank!"

Mark Zupo

"As an authority, you don't have to earn the right to get paid.

In a doctor's office you might drop your shorts....

In a dentist office...you don't!"

Mark Zupo

"You may be disappointed if you fail, but you are doomed if you don't try."

Mark Zupo

"If it's done on time its education...

If it's done later...its therapy."

Unknown

"You have to Learn-2-Earn"

"What college doesn't teach you about making your fortune,

life will measure you by how you never made a fortune."

Mark Zupo

"People can be divided into three groups:
Those who *make* things happen
Those who *watch* things happen and
Those who *wonder* what happened."

John W. Newbern

"The obstacles to success are not

the things we think we need to be successful,

It's getting rid of the things that

we have that get in the way of our success."

Mark Zupo

"Every drop of water is just as wet as any other drop of water."

Mark Zupo

"Just because you are sharing a moment in time with someone else
doesn't mean that you are having the same experience."...just ask my wife!

Mark Zupo

"Do not judge people by their size, shape, color, beliefs and intentions. We are all different and yet the same. Ice cream comes in different flavors...

it's still ice cream."

Mark Zupo

"Rocks need polishing to become gems.

Gems need polishing regularly to remain brilliant."

Mark Zupo

"A diamond in an ugly setting is still a diamond."

Mark Zupo

"Let your attitude be your latitude."

Kanye West

"Do more to get more!"

George Hedley

"Your life is Big Business...and someone should teach you how to run it like one"

Mark Zupo

"Success can be a problem...
If you don't question it then how can you solve for it?"

Mark Zupo

"Just because it's out of reach only means that you have to stretch to get it."

Mark Zupo

"Imagination is more valuable than knowledge."

Albert Einstein

"The one thing that interferes with learning is education."

Albert Einstein

"The only way to make a mistake is to try something new and...if you have never made a mistake then you aren't trying hard enough!"

Albert Einstein

"Wealth can only be achieved by understanding it."

Mark Zupo

"Curiosity exists to question everything."

Mark Zupo

"What college doesn't teach you...
life will?"

Mark Zupo

"You can't get up until you look up"

Mark Zupo

“Man makes the money, money doesn’t make the Man”

Mark Zupo

'People that think that money is bad...don’t have any!"

Mark Zupo

"Poor people have big televisions

Rich people have big libraries."

Mark Zupo

"If all that you see is the payment you'll never see the pay-off."

Mark Zupo

"Think that you're wrong...

Think that you're right...

Either way...you're right."

Henry Ford

"If you're not making mistakes...
then you're sleeping."

Mark Zupo

"Failure is the major contributor to success."

Mark Zupo

"If one seeks to become a speaker before men, one must first learn to listen to women"

Mark Zupo

"Think like a winner and

Act like a champion"

Mark Zupo

"Early to bed and early to rise...

Work like Hell and advertise!

Ted Turner

The cure for sanity is creativity

Albert Einstein

A champion will always go one more round

Rocky Balboa

A person's worth to society is measured by their wealth when in fact their wealth should be measured by their worth to society.

Mark Zupo

"No pressure...No diamonds!"

Mark Zupo

The only constant is change

Heraclitus

Enthusiasm is transferrable

Ralph Waldo Emerson

I believe in luck...

The harder I work the more I have.

Thomas Jefferson

"The definition of
Success"

Insert your picture here ---

A note from Mark

Hello and welcome!

First I would like to say thank you for your trust. I know there is a world of options out there but you chose my book. That is a very humbling and special thing for me.

I am an entrepreneur who has published books, created online home study courses, created digital information books, mentor, trained and presented at various seminars both in-person and online. For the past 24 years I have been actively involved with mentoring in the success-motivation industry.

As a thought-leader and business mentor, I have worked with businesses and people all over the world. I have worked with educators, business owners, individuals, entrepreneurs, lawyers, consultants, coaches, trainers and more. As founder of the ***7Level Success Academy***® I have helped these same people achieve personal and business success, improvement to life and happiness. This is my passion. This is my purpose!

"Make Your Business Your Life and Make Your Life Your Business!"
- Mark Zupo

A final thought for my friends:

I cherish my friends with greater value than anything I own or hold in my possession. I well understand that friendship is not something I can demand but must earn. It is you, my friends, that define who I am, what I am and what I will be. I hope to count you as the best of friends.

"Friends are like old shoes, you wear them, walk on them, abuse them, kick them around and throw them in a corner...but you hold on to them and never throw them out because it took years for them to fit just right."

Mark Zupo

Conclusion

We all understand, regardless of where we are in life, no matter what business or industry we entertain, that we are in the people business. What differentiates us from the masses is that we understand that we are also in the ME business too. We have spent our entire lifetime building, educating, improving, detailing, sharpening, motivating, strengthening and training ourselves to be the finest product ever to hit the market. You have improved on the invention of YOU in every way until you have become the tool of choice in your business and industry.

The truest business YOU have ever worked in is the business of your life, and you have never been paid your real value and your real worth. It is time that you be rewarded for a lifetime of labor and attention. The product of YOU is ready and waiting to be unleashed on the world, and now is the time.

The obstacles to success are not the things we think we lack to be successful; the true obstacle is getting rid of the things that we have that get in the way of our success. Successful people do what other people don't want to do.

To Your Success...

100 Quotes I Live By

Opportunity

Don't Spend Years Trying to Write Your Book!

There is a Fast and Painless Way to Write a Book without Having to Actually Write it Word for Word!

The Secrets to Writing & Selling Your First Book Fast are within reach in:

The Original How to "Write and Sell Your First Book" Workshop

You have always thought of writing a book, but you just can't find the time, right? Now you can...because I will show you how to do it faster than you ever thought possible!

The **"YourFastBook™"** Workshop will give you all the tools you'll ever need to "blast" out a book in no time flat!

In the "YourFastBook™" workshop, you'll learn:

- How to write your book without ever putting pen to paper!
- How to market your book without ever paying a publisher!

- How to make your book available to millions with a click of a button!
- How to avoid the 10 most common mistakes authors make!
- How to protect your copyright with this simple free technique!
- How never to pay a royalty keeping all the profit for yourself!

Still Not Convinced?

I am the author or co-author of more-than 23 books to date. I am a "top-selling" author and credible authority on the self-publishing secrets that the conventional industry publishers don't want to you to know.

Check this out! When you enroll in my award-winning workshop you'll get all this and more:

- ✓ How to compose your book in one day!
- ✓ How to give your book an award-winning title!
- ✓ The three secrets to every author's success with future orders!
- ✓ How to turn your book into a "Money-Machine."
- ✓ How to make people pay five times what you paid for printing!
- ✓ How to develop multiple streams of income from your book.

You MUST get in on this workshop right NOW!

Classes fill up quickly, so sign-up now and become a self-published author!

Workshop Details:

Become an author and wow your friends and relatives. Start your book now by enrolling in this exclusive workshop today!

Turn your computer into your personal "ATM".

See what other authors say about the YourFastBook™ workshop.

"Unbelievable! What could be more fun than writing a book that becomes your signature trademark? I am really proud to be a part of this seminar and see just what anyone could do with the information that they already had. Writing a book is more fun than I ever imagined. I was absolutely amazed at the speed at which I can write a book when I thought that it would take years to complete."

"I could never have imagined that I could be a published author until I met Mark Zupo. He allowed me to think on a different level about traditional publishing. I am now a self-publishing advocate forever!"

"When I enrolled in Mark's workshop, I was skeptical and reserved to think that I had a book in me that someone would want to read. Now I know that my story is as powerful as any book that has ever been written. I am empowered as a new author to help other people write their story too."

"I've always felt I had a book within me. Years

ago, I wanted to be a children's book author. I even took a well-known children's literature course I saw advertised in a magazine, and for which I paid dearly. Rejection slips kept coming back after sending in my queries to traditional publishing companies. I finally said, "To heck with this," and packed all my thoughts and papers away.

"Then, I met Mark. His enthusiasm and down-right sincerity convinced me I could create my own book. Now, I'm a published author! I would not hesitate to tell everyone to take Mark's course. Not only does he know what he's talking about, but he has the proof to back it up."

Are you too far away from Atlanta?

Choose the One-on-One Book *e*Conference Package with Mark Zupo

The Executive Author Conference:

- **eConference 1:** We will nail down the focus of your book, the title and niche the market wants and needs, and the idea and synopsis. Then we'll devise a plan for writing, printing, marketing and self-publishing it. We will tailor your personal objectives and timeline for completion of the book content. I will give you some of the resources for the writing, printing and publishing you will need at this stage.

- **eConference 2:** Here we will evaluate the content of your book and formulate questions and the answers that will deliver the information that will become chapters. We'll talk about the process of establishing a brand, finding a market, positioning your book for discovery and creating methods of future income from your book.

- **eConference 3:** In this session we bring together the content, the format and the completeness of the book. We discuss income streams and methods for future books. At this stage we can start to see the results of the book in real life.

Note: We will schedule three one-hour, one-on-one conferences

(via Freeconferencecall.com, iChat, Skype or telephone). Also, there will be 2-3 additional hours of discussion via email to unite your work with the industry standard for what a book must contain.

The purpose of this package is to focus your idea and material into a print-ready product to begin your life as a self-published author.

This package is not for people who sit around and talk about how hard it is to write a book! **This package is a proven method of self-publishing.** This is your opportunity to be a self-published author with lightning speed!

SCHEDULE **YOURFASTBOOK™ Executive eConference** now!

About the Author

Mark Zupo is an "Accomplished Entrepreneur" who has devoted his life to helping others succeed in their goals and dreams. His goal is to help you fulfill your career goals and achieve financial freedom and independence by managing a successful virtual business. Because he has worked in the e-commerce business, his consulting and e-Business acumen remains unequaled as an *Entrepreneurial Authority*. Mark is a leader, entrepreneur and mentor to many.

Mark says, "I'm a kid at heart! I believe in having a good time and working hard. I'm fortunate to have an unbelievably supportive family and many great friends. I describe myself as a "workaholic, serial-entrepreneur, and innovative-geek sort of guy. I have been fortunate to have realized almost all of my dreams."

Mark Zupo is a dynamic and insightful speaker, recognized for his empowering and motivational focus to your success. As a driven leader with a commanding presence, he motivates, inspires, energizes and empowers his audience.

Mark Zupo has been the driving force in changing the lives of anyone within range of his voice. Mark's "3-Foot Rule" makes him one of the most sought-after speakers in his industry.

Mark Zupo

Mark's Books:

1. **"You Deserve to be Rich"**
   The Secrets to Earning What You're Really Worth

2. **From Mess to Millionaire**
   One Man's Story of Failure to Success

3. **Speak for Yourself**
   The 7-Secrets of How to Make your Living Speaking

4. **Dean of the DUMP!**
   What I Learned When I lived at the Garbage Dump!

5. **Mind Your Business**
   How to Re-Package your Life Experience

6. **Leadership**
   From Ability to Credibility

7. **Achieve what You Believe**
   Finding Dynamic Success in Self-empowerment

8. **7-Level Millionaire**
   Freedom, Independence & Liberty

Sources and Resources

Mark's speaking career in industry spans 25 years. He has delivered more-than, 1,200 presentations. From his experiences he has authored and co-authored many books on self-development, business development techniques and marketing enterprises. Mark speaks on several topics that enlighten, entertain and motivate his audiences to action!

Mark's Most Requested Topics/Programs:

- **My Adversity University**

"Build Power, Credibility and Respect from Life's Lessons"

- **Champion Your Success**

"Achieve What You Believe, Believe What You Can Achieve'

- **7-Secrets of Business Success**

"The Keys to Wealth and Freedom"

- **Leadership**

"From Ability to Credibility"

Schedule Mark to Speak at Your Next Event!
Contact us: 1-678-640-0585
09:00 – 5:00 EST

On-line: *www.MarkZupo.com*
markzupo@gmail.com

www.7LevelSuccess.com

www.MarkZupo.com

DISCLAIMER

contents within are accurate, due to the rapidly changing nature of the business. However, there may be mistakes in typography or content. The purpose of this e-book is to educate.

While all attempts have been made to verify information provided in this publication, the publisher assumes no responsibility for errors, omissions, or contrary interpretation of the subject matter herein. Any perceived slights of specific persons, peoples, or organizations are unintentional.

This book is a common-sense guide to marketing online. In practical advice books, like in anything else in life, there are no guarantees of income made. Readers are cautioned to reply with their own judgment about their individual circumstances and to act accordingly. This book is not intended for use as a source of legal, business, accounting or financial advice. All readers are advised to seek services of competent professionals in legal, business, accounting and finance fields.

This information is presented for educational and informational purposes only and is not intended to be a substitute for professional advice. Never disregard professional advice or delay in seeking it because of something read or heard.

We make every effort to ensure that we accurately represent our products and services and their potential for income. Earning and income statements made by our company and its customers are estimates of what we think you can possibly earn. There is no guarantee that you will make the level of income you desire, and you accept the risk that the earnings and income statements differ by individual.

As with any business, your results may vary and will be based on your individual capacity, business experience, expertise, and level of desire. The testimonials and examples used are exceptional results, which do not apply to the average purchaser, and are not intended to represent or guarantee that anyone will achieve the same or similar results. Each individual's success depends on his or her background, dedication, desire and motivation.

The use of our information, products and services should be based on your own due diligence, and you hold harmless our company for any success or failure of your business that is directly or indirectly related to the purchase and use of our information, products and services.

"Yesterday is history...Tomorrow is a mystery, Today is a gift, which is why it is called the "Present"...

Live for today as though tomorrow never comes!

- **Eleanor Roosevelt**

100 Quotes I Live By

Made in the USA
Monee, IL
04 November 2026

67387222R00075